GIRL, IT'S TIME TO HEAL

Copyright © 2024 Adrianne Michelle Spain

All rights reserved. No part of this publication may be reproduced, distributed, or transmitted in any form or by any means, including photocopying, recording, or other electronic or mechanical methods, without the prior written permission of the publisher, except in the case of brief quotations embodied in critical reviews and certain other noncommercial uses permitted by copyright law. For permission requests, write to the publisher, addressed "Attention: Permissions Coordinator," at the address below.

Paperback ISBN: 978-1-63616-222-5

Published By Opportune Independent Publishing Co.
www.opportunepublishing.com

Printed in the United States of America

For permission requests, please email the publisher with the subject line as "Attention: Permissions Coordinator"
to the email address below:
Info@Opportunepublishing.com

Table of Contents

Dedication
Acknowledgment
Introduction

   1. Kelly & Corey
      Betrayal, Healing and New Beginning

   2. Lover
      Love, Faith and Temptation

   3. Rounds of Love
      Toxic Relationships, Self-Worth, Unhealthy Love and Growth

   4. God's Plan
      Protection, Influence and Moving Forward

   5. Broken Promises
      Healing

   6. Best Friend
      Reflecting on Friendship

   7. Mom & Dad
      Acknowledging Pain and Addiction

   8. Puppies
      Trauma, Shame and Sexual Assault

   9. Phat Girl
      Self-Worth and Body Image

   10. Family Secret
      Reflecting on Past

   11. Keep Dreaming
      Rediscover Your Dream and Embrace Your Gift

Dedication

To all the strong sisters who have faced the storms of life head-on, Whether you've battled trauma, endured broken hearts, struggled with weight issues or wrestled with self-esteem, whether you've faced relationship problems, shame, body energy challenges or the deep wounds of sexual abuse — this workbook is for you.

Either you've overcome or you're still on your journey of healing. No matter where you are, this is your reminder: Girl, breathe again. I dedicate this book to you, in honor of your strength and resilience.

Acknowledgment

First and foremost, I want to give thanks to God for giving me the strength, vision and guidance to bring this workbook to life. It has been a journey, and I couldn't have done it alone.

To everyone who has supported me throughout this process — whether through words of encouragement, prayers or simply standing by me — I am deeply grateful. Your love and support mean the world, and while I can't name everyone individually, please know that my heart is full of gratitude for each of you.

A special thanks to Shamaro Clayton, Adrienne Tucker, Ronnice Little-Barnes, and my incredible assistant, Juanita McCoy. Your unwavering support and dedication made this workbook come together in record-breaking time. You all were a constant source of strength and motivation, and I couldn't have done it without you.

I am forever grateful to my mother, Brenda Spain, for her love, wisdom and encouragement throughout my life. To my spiritual parents, Apostle Bryan Andrew Wilson and Prophetess Tiffany Wilson — thank you for your guidance and covering throughout this journey. Your prayers and mentorship have been a blessing.

A heartfelt thank you to Dr. Stephanie Mitchell from Quincy, Florida, for your kindness and wisdom. Your support has meant so much to me.

And last but certainly not least, to my three children — Rashad, Victor Christian, and Brenda — thank you for being my inspiration and my joy. You are the reason I continue to push forward, and I love you more than words can express.

Introduction

A Journey of Healing, Growth and Rediscovery
Life has a way of testing us in ways we never expected. The pain of betrayal, the struggles with temptation and the weight of toxic relationships can leave us feeling trapped in cycles of unhealthy love and low self-worth. Trauma, shame and abuse add layers to this brokenness, often distorting how we see ourselves and the world around us. But this workbook is designed to help you confront those wounds and embrace healing, understanding that God's plan is far greater than the pain of your past.

We will walk together through the difficult emotions tied to betrayal and loss, helping you reflect on your friendships and relationships. What influences — whether from people, culture or past experiences — have shaped how you see yourself today? As you examine these influences, you will be encouraged to confront the pain, not in isolation but with faith. With God's guidance, we can start the journey toward new beginnings, repairing old wounds and embracing the future with renewed hope and confidence.

Understanding Your Worth in Love and Faith

One of the greatest battles we face is understanding our self-worth. Many of us have been in relationships where we were not valued or loved as we deserved. Perhaps we've stayed in toxic environments because we believed we couldn't do better or were afraid of being alone. But this workbook will help you reclaim your worth. Through faith, you'll come to realize that your value doesn't come from others' approval or love but from God, who created you with purpose and intention.

We will explore what healthy love looks like — love that builds you up rather than tears you down. With every page, you'll find the tools to break free from the unhealthy love that has harmed you and embrace the love that nourishes your soul. God's love offers protection and wisdom, and through it, you'll learn to protect your heart, guard your boundaries and nurture relationships that honor your self-worth.

Overcoming Weight Struggles

Weight issues often tie into our self-worth as well. Whether through unhealthy eating habits, emotional eating or physical struggles, our bodies can carry the weight of emotional pain. This journey of healing will help you embrace the process of caring for your body, overcoming negative body image and developing healthy habits that reflect how precious you are in God's eyes. We'll explore how physical health is connected to emotional well-being and how small, intentional steps can lead to big transformations over time.

Moving Forward: Embracing Growth and Rediscovering Dreams
The process of healing and self-discovery isn't just about addressing the pain—it's about moving forward and embracing new opportunities for growth. There's beauty in new beginnings, and as you work through this workbook, you'll rediscover dreams that you thought were lost. Whether it's a dream to pursue a new career, reignite a forgotten passion or step into a new role that reflects your gifts, this is a time for rediscovery.

Part of this growth is learning to reflect on the past without being controlled by it. You'll learn to acknowledge past pain, trauma and shame but not let them define you. Instead, you'll reflect with purpose—extracting wisdom from those experiences and using it to propel you forward into a future marked by strength, resilience and faith.

Encouragement
As you begin this workbook, I want to remind you that healing is not linear. There will be moments of progress and setbacks, but every step you take is a step closer to becoming the person God designed you to be. Embrace the journey. Take your time to reflect, pray and journal through each section, knowing that you are not alone. God's love is with you, guiding you through every challenge and triumph.

This is your time to heal, to grow, to rebuild. It's your time to rediscover your dreams, reclaim your self-worth and embrace the gifts that are uniquely yours. Let's walk this path together, knowing that with faith, perseverance and God's grace, all things are possible.

Chapter 1: Kelly & Corey
REFLECTIONS ON BETRAYAL, HEALING AND NEW BEGINNINGS

> **Processing Betrayal**
> *Matthew 6:14–15: "In prayer there is a connection between what God does and what you do. You can't get forgiveness from God, for instance, without also forgiving others. If you refuse to do your part, you cut yourself off from God's part."*

How has betrayal affected you emotionally and spiritually?

_____
_____
_____

Why is it important to forgive those who have hurt you, and what steps can you take to forgive?

_____
_____
_____

> **Healing and Letting Go**
> *Psalm 147:3: "He heals the heartbroken and bandages their wounds."*

What does healing look like for me after this experience?

_____
_____
_____

How can I release feelings of resentment and move forward in peace?

_____

_____

_____

> ***Rebuilding Trust***
> *Jeremiah 17:7: "But blessed is the man who trusts in me, God, the woman who sticks with God."*

What can I learn from this situation about trust?

_____

_____

_____

How can I rebuild trust in future relationships while protecting my heart?

_____

_____

_____

> ***Learning from the Past***
> *Romans 8:28: "That's why we can be so sure that every detail in our lives of love for God is worked into something good."*

What valuable lessons have I learned from this relationship?

_____

_____

_____

How can I use these lessons to create healthier relationships in the future?

_____

_____

_____

> **Moving Toward New Beginnings**
> *Isaiah 43:18-19: "Forget about what's happened; Don't keep going over old history. Be alert, be present. I'm about to do something brand new. It's bursting out! Don't you see it?"*

What positive steps can I take toward building a better future?

_____

_____

_____

How can I rely on God's guidance as I move forward?

_____

_____

_____

Reflection

How has this experience deepened my relationship with God and strengthened my faith?

_____
_____
_____
_____

Prayer

Write a prayer to thank God for His healing and guidance, asking for continued strength as you move into a new season of life.

_____
_____
_____
_____

Prayer

Heavenly Father,
In the midst of the pain caused by betrayal, I come to You for comfort and strength. Heal my heart from the wounds of broken trust, and help me release the bitterness that tries to take root. Renew my spirit with Your peace and guide me toward forgiveness, even when it feels impossible.

Lord, as You heal me, I ask for the courage to embrace new beginnings. Lead me into fresh opportunities and relationships filled with love, honesty and grace. I trust Your plan for my future and know that with You, I will rise stronger and restored.
In Jesus' name,
Amen.

GIRL, IT'S TIME TO HEAL

GIRL, IT'S TIME TO HEAL

Chapter 2: Lovers
LOVE, FAITH AND TEMPTATION

> **Guarding Your Heart in Relationships**
> *Proverbs 4:23: "Keep vigilant watch over your heart; that's where life starts."*

What does it mean to guard your heart in relationships?

_____
_____
_____

How can faith guide your choices in love?

_____
_____
_____

> *2 Corinthians 6:14: "Don't become partners with those who reject God."*

Have you ever compromised your beliefs for someone you loved?

_____
_____
_____

How did it impact your relationship with God?

_____
_____
_____

> **Mr. Unforgettable: Regret and Maturity**
> *Proverbs 19:20: "Take good counsel and accept correction—that's the way to live wisely and well."*

How has hindsight changed your view of past relationships?

_____
_____
_____

What lessons can you carry into the future?

_____
_____
_____

The Encounter with the Demon: Spiritual Warfare

_____
_____
_____

> *Ephesians 6:12:* "*This is no weekend war that we'll walk away from and forget about in a couple of hours. This is for keeps, a life or death fight to finish against the devil and all his angels.*"

Have you ever experienced spiritual attacks?

_____
_____
_____

How do you strengthen yourself in God's armor?

_____
_____
_____

Adultery and Forgiveness: Repentance and Redemption

_____
_____
_____

> *1 John 1:9:* "*On the other hand, if we admit our sins, simply come clean about them, He won't let us down. He'll be true to himself. He'll forgive our sins and purge us of all wrongdoing.*"

How do you reconcile with God after falling into temptation?

_____
_____
_____

How does His grace shape your journey?

_____
_____
_____

> **The Ugly Duckling: Discernment and God's Timing**
> *Isaiah 40:31: "But those who wait upon God get fresh strength..."*

How can you discern whether someone is truly from God?

_____
_____
_____

How do you remain patient and trust God's timing in relationships?

_____
_____
_____

> **Trusting God in Relationships: Obedience to God's Plan**
> *Jeremiah 29:11: "I know what I'm doing. I have it all planned out; plans to take care of you, not abandon you, plans to give you the future you hope for."*

What steps can you take to better align your relationship decisions with God's plan for your life?

_____

_____

_____

> **Growth Through Grace**
> *Psalm 37:4: "Keep company with God, get in on the best."*

How has God's grace shaped your understanding of love and relationships?

_____

_____

_____

Prayer

Write a prayer asking for wisdom and discernment in future relationships.

_____

_____

_____

_____

_____

Prayer

Gracious God,

I come before You seeking Your love to fill my heart and heal the places where I've been hurt. Strengthen my faith, so I may trust in Your goodness even in moments of doubt. When I am tempted to stray from Your path or give in to weakness, remind me of Your promises and keep me grounded in Your truth.

Help me to grow in love for others and for myself, trusting that Your grace is sufficient to carry me through every trial. Let Your peace rest upon me as I walk in faith and overcome the struggles before me.
In Jesus' name,
Amen.

GIRL, IT'S TIME TO HEAL

GIRL, IT'S TIME TO HEAL

Chapter 3: Rounds of Love
JOURNEY OF HEALING AND GROWTH

> *Jeremiah 29:11:* "*I know what I'm doing. I have it all planned out; plans to take care of you, not abandon you, plans to give you the future you hope for.*"

What is the purpose of this journal for you?

_____
_____
_____

How have past relationships and God's grace impacted your journey?

_____
_____
_____

> **Self-Worth and Identity**
> *Song of Songs 4:7:* "*You're beautiful from head to toe, my dear love, beautiful beyond compare, absolutely flawless.*"

How do you define your self-worth today?

_____
_____
_____

How does that reflect what God says about you?

_____
_____
_____

> **Recognizing Toxic Relationships**
> *Proverbs 4:23: "Keep vigilant watch over your heart; that's where life starts."*

Have you ever mistaken possessiveness or control for love?

_____
_____
_____

How did that impact your self-worth?

_____
_____
_____

> **Breaking Cycles of Unhealthy Love**
> *Romans 12:2: "Don't become so well adjusted to your culture that you fit into it without even thinking. Instead, fix your attention on God. You'll be changed from the inside out…"*

What patterns of behavior in relationships do you need to break?

_____
_____
_____

Why have these patterns continued?

_____
_____
_____

> **Healing from Abuse**
> *Psalm 9:9: "God's a safe house for the battered, a sanctuary during bad times."*

Have you ever normalized abuse or minimized it?

_____
_____
_____

How has that affected you emotionally and spiritually?

_____
_____
_____

Forgiving Yourself
Romans 8:1: "Those who enter into Christ being here for us no longer have to live under a continuous, low-lying black cloud."

How does your past affect your ability to forgive yourself?

_____
_____
_____

What would you say to a friend who experienced what you did?

_____
_____
_____

God's Grace and Redemption
Romans 5:8: "But God put his love on the line for us by offering his son in sacrificial death while we were of no use whatever to him."

When have you felt God's grace in your life?

_____
_____
_____

GIRL, IT'S TIME TO HEAL

How has it changed your perspective on love?

_____
_____
_____

> **Moving Forward in Love**
> Colossians 3:14: *"And regardless of what else you put on, wear love. It's your basic, all-purpose garment. Never be without it."*

What does a healthy, Christ-centered relationship look like for you?

_____
_____
_____

How does it differ from your past relationships?

_____
_____
_____

> **Celebrating Your Growth**
> Ephesians 2:10: *"He creates each of us by Christ Jesus to join him in the work he does, the good work he has gotten ready for us to do, work we had better be doing."*

What is one lesson you've learned from your journey?

_____
_____
_____

How will you carry this lesson forward?

_____

_____

_____

> *Proverbs 3:5–6: "Trust God from the bottom of your heart; don't try to figure out everything on your own. Listen for God's voice in everything you do, everywhere you go; He's the one who will keep you on track."*

How will you continue to trust God with your heart moving forward?

_____

_____

_____

A Prayer for Healing and Restoration

Heavenly Father,
Thank You for walking with me on this journey of healing, growth and self-discovery. I come before You with a heart open to Your love and grace. As I reflect on the experiences that have shaped me, I ask for Your continued guidance and strength. Lord, help me to release any guilt or shame I may carry and replace it with the truth of Your forgiveness. Where there has been hurt, bring healing; where there has been brokenness, bring restoration. Let Your love wash over me, cleansing my spirit and renewing my mind. Teach me to value myself the way You do, and help me to recognize my worth as Your child. Guide me in my future relationships so that I may honor You in my choices and actions. Help me to guard my heart, trust in Your plan and seek only the love that reflects Your own. Thank You for never leaving me, even in my darkest moments. I place my past, present and future in Your hands, knowing that You will continue to lead me on the path of healing, love and wholeness.
In Jesus' name, I pray,
Amen.

GIRL, IT'S TIME TO HEAL

GIRL, IT'S TIME TO HEAL

Chapter 4: God's Plan
GOD'S PLAN FOR YOU

1. When have you felt God's hand guiding you, even if you didn't recognize it at the time?

_____
_____
_____

2. Are there any areas in your life where you have strayed from God's path? What caused you to drift?

_____
_____
_____

> **The Power of God's Protection**
> *Jeremiah 29:11: "I know what I'm doing. I have it all planned out; plans to take care of you, not abandon you, plans to give you the future you hope for."*

1. Have there been moments in your life where you realized later that God was protecting you?

_____
_____
_____

2. How does knowing that God is always watching over you change the way you live?

_____
_____
_____

> **The Influence of Others**
> *Psalm 91:11: "He ordered his angels to guard you where you go."*

Reflection Questions:

1. Who has influenced your spiritual journey? How did they impact your relationship with God?

_____
_____
_____

2. How can you be a positive influence on someone else's spiritual journey?

_____
_____
_____

> **Struggles and Temptations**
> *Proverbs 22:6:* "Point your kids in the right direction; when they're old, they won't be lost."

What are the main temptations or distractions that have drawn you away from God?

_____

_____

_____

How can you begin to resist these temptations and turn back to God?

_____

_____

_____

> **Turning Back to God**
> *1 Corinthians 10:13:* "No test or temptation that comes your way is beyond the course of what others have had to face. All you need to remember is that God will never let you down; He'll never let you be pushed past your limit; He'll always be there to help you come through it."

What was your turning point when you felt the need to come back to God?

_____

_____

_____

How has your life changed since turning back to God?

_____
_____
_____

> **God's Call for Your Life**
> *Luke 15:7: "Count on it; there's more joy in heaven over one sinner's rescued life than over 99 good people in no need of rescue."*

Do you feel that God is calling you to something specific? What is it?

_____
_____
_____

What are the challenges that are preventing you from fully accepting God's call?

_____
_____
_____

> **Moving Forward in Faith**
> *Isaiah 6:8: "And then I heard the voice of the Master, 'Whom shall I send? Who will go for us?' I spoke up, 'I'll go. Send me!'"*

What steps can you take to strengthen your relationship with God moving forward?

_____

_____

_____

How can you begin to walk more confidently in the calling God has for you?

_____

_____

_____

> *Philippians 1:6: "There has never been the slightest doubt in my mind that the God who started this great work in you will keep at it and bring it to a flourishing finish on the very day Christ Jesus appears."*

Reflect on the unmet promises in your life. How did these experiences affect you emotionally and spiritually?

_____

_____

_____

> *Psalm 27:10: "My father and mother walked out and left me, but God took me in."*

Consider what it means to have God as a Father. How has God filled the void left by the absence or inconsistency of your earthly father?

_____

_____

_____

> *2 Corinthians 6:18: "'I'll be a Father to you; you'll be sons and daughters to me.' The word of the Master, God."*

Acknowledge patterns from your biological father that you may have unknowingly repeated. What steps can you take to break these cycles?

_____

_____

_____

Disappointment often leads to emotional scars that affect trust. What are some ways you can rebuild trust in relationships, both with others and with God?

_____

_____

_____

> *Proverbs 3:5–6: "Trust God from the bottom of your heart; don't try to figure out everything on your own. Listen for God's voice in everything you do, everywhere you go; He's the one who will keep you on track."*

Father wounds can have deep impacts, but God offers healing and restoration. Reflect on how God has begun to heal those places in your heart.

_____

_____

_____

Forgiveness is essential for moving forward. What steps can you take to forgive your father and anyone else who has hurt you?

_____

_____

_____

> *Colossians 3:13: "Be even-tempered, content with second place, quick to forgive an offense. Forgive as quickly and completely as the Master forgave you."*

How have you allowed your identity to be shaped by your relationship with your father? How can you shift your focus to your identity in Christ?

_____

_____

_____

What promises from God do you need to cling to right now? How can you remind yourself of these promises daily?

_____

_____

_____

Prayers

Heavenly Father,
I thank You for being my perfect Father, for loving me unconditionally and for never abandoning me. I bring before You the hurt and disappointment I have felt from broken promises and unmet expectations. Help me to forgive those who have hurt me, including my earthly father. Heal the deep wounds in my heart and restore my trust in You and in others.

Thank You for breaking every generational curse and unhealthy pattern in my life. Help me to live out my identity in Christ and to lean on Your promises daily. I ask that You continue to guide me in this journey of healing, freedom and growth.
In Jesus' name, I pray,
Amen.

Heavenly Father,
Thank You for Your protection, guidance and love throughout my life. Even when I have strayed, You have always called me back to Your arms. Lord, I ask that You continue to guide me on this journey of faith. Give me the strength to resist temptation and the wisdom to follow the calling You have placed on my heart.

I surrender my life to You, Lord, trusting that Your plan is greater than anything I could imagine. Help me walk in obedience and faith, knowing that You will never leave me nor forsake me. Thank You for Your forgiveness, grace and unfailing love.
In Jesus' name,
Amen.

GIRL, IT'S TIME TO HEAL

GIRL, IT'S TIME TO HEAL

Chapter 5: Broken Promises
HEALING PATTERN, CYCLES, DISAPPOINTMENT AND UNFORGIVENESS

> ***Identifying the Wounds of Abandonment***
> *Psalm 27:10: "My father and mother walked out on me, but God took me in."*

Reflect on the unmet promises in your life. How did these experiences affect you emotionally and spiritually?

_____

_____

_____

Write about a time when you felt abandoned or let down. How did it affect your view of yourself and your relationship with others?

_____

_____

_____

> ***Fatherhood Through God's Eyes***
> *2 Corinthians 6:18: "I'll be a Father to you; you'll be sons and daughters to me. The word of the Master, God."*

Consider what it means to have God as a Father. How has God filled the void left by the absence or inconsistency of your earthly father?

_____

_____

_____

Write about how you have experienced God's fatherhood in your life. What do you believe a perfect father should be like?

_____

_____

_____

> **Generational Patterns and Breaking Cycles**
> *Ezekiel 18:20: "The child does not share the guilt of the parent, nor does the parent the guilt of the child..."*

Acknowledge patterns from your biological father that you may have unknowingly repeated. Pray for the strength to break these cycles.

_____

_____

_____

Write down any unhealthy patterns you recognize in yourself that may have been passed down through your father or family line. What steps can you take to break these cycles?

_____

_____

_____

> **Dealing with Disappointment**
> *Proverbs 3:5-6:* "Trust God from the bottom of your heart; don't try to figure out everything on your own. Listen for God's voice in everything you do, everywhere you go; He's the one who will keep you on track."

Disappointment often leads to emotional scars that affect trust. What are some ways you can rebuild trust in relationships, both with others and with God?

_____

_____

_____

How do you cope with disappointment? What has helped you heal from broken promises in your life?

_____

_____

_____

> **Healing from Father Wounds**
> *Psalm 147:3:* "He heals the heartbroken and bandages their wounds."

Father wounds can have deep impacts, but God offers healing and restoration. Reflect on how God has begun to heal those places in your heart.

_____

_____

_____

In what areas of your life do you need healing from your relationship with your father? How has God shown His healing power to you?

_____

_____

_____

> **Forgiveness – A Path to Freedom**
> *Colossians 3:13:* "Be even-tempered, content with second place, quick to forgive an offense. Forgive as quickly and completely as the Master forgave you."

Forgiveness is essential for moving forward. What steps can you take to forgive your father and anyone else who has hurt you?

_____

_____

_____

Write a letter to your father (or father figure) expressing your feelings. Include words of forgiveness, even if you don't feel ready to send it.

_____
_____
_____

> **Rediscovering Identity in Christ**
> Ephesians 1:5: "Long, long ago, He decided to adopt us into His family through Jesus Christ." (What pleasure He took in planning this!)

Your identity is not defined by the actions or absence of your father but by who you are in Christ.

_____
_____
_____

How have you allowed your identity to be shaped by your relationship with your father? How can you shift your focus to your identity in Christ?

_____
_____
_____

> **Embracing God's Promises**
> 2 Peter 3:9: "God isn't late with his promise as some measure lateness. He is restraining himself on account of you, holding back the end because He doesn't want anyone lost. He's giving everyone space and time to change."

God never breaks His promises. Reflect on the promises God has made to you in His Word and how they bring hope and restoration.

_____
_____
_____

What promises from God do you need to cling to right now? How can you remind yourself of these promises daily?

_____
_____
_____
_____
_____

Prayer

Heavenly Father,
I thank You for being my perfect Father, for loving me unconditionally, and for never abandoning me. I bring before You the hurt and disappointment I have felt from broken promises and unmet expectations. Help me to forgive those who have hurt me, including my earthly father. Heal the deep wounds in my heart and restore my trust in You and in others.

Thank You for breaking every generational curse and unhealthy pattern in my life. Help me to live out my identity in Christ and to lean on Your promises daily. I ask that You continue to guide me in this journey of healing, freedom and growth.
In Jesus' name, I pray.
Amen.

GIRL, IT'S TIME TO HEAL

GIRL, IT'S TIME TO HEAL

Chapter 6: Best Friend
REFLECTING ON THE FRIENDSHIP

> *Proverbs 17:17 (NIV): "Friends love through all kinds of weather, and families stick together in all kinds of trouble."*

Think about the beginning of your friendship. What made the relationship special?

_____
_____
_____
_____

How did you support each other?

_____
_____
_____
_____

Describe the foundation of your friendship. What made you feel close to your friend?

_____
_____
_____
_____

> ***Recognizing the Break***
> *Ephesians 4:31–32 (NIV): "Make a clean break with all cutting, backbiting, profane talk. Be gentle with one another, sensitive. Forgive one another as quickly and thoroughly as God in Christ forgave you."*

Time to think about it.
Acknowledge the moment when the friendship began to change.

What emotions did you experience?

_____

_____

_____

Write about the breaking point in the friendship. How did it affect you emotionally?

_____

_____

_____

> ***Understanding Miscommunication***
> *Proverbs 18:24: "Friends come and friends go, but a true friend sticks by you like family."*

Reflection: Misunderstandings can often lead to fractures in relationships. Reflect on any miscommunication or assumptions that may have contributed to the break.

What role did communication (or lack thereof) play in the breakdown of your friendship?

_____

_____

_____

_____

> **The Power of Forgiveness**
> *Colossians 3:13: "Be even-tempered, content with second place, quick to forgive an offense. Forgive as quickly and completely as the Master forgave you."*

Forgiveness is a choice, not just for the other person but also for your own healing. Reflect on your ability to forgive and let go of past hurt.

_____

_____

_____

_____

Write about what it would mean to forgive your friend. What feelings do you need to release in order to heal?

_____

_____

_____

_____

> *James 5:16: "Make this your common practice: confess your sins to each other and pray for each other so that you can live together whole and healed. The prayer of a person living right with God is something powerful to be reckoned with."*

Prayer is a powerful tool for healing and reconciliation. End this section with a heartfelt prayer for your friend and for yourself.

Prayer Prompt: Write a prayer asking for healing, understanding and the grace to move forward with love and forgiveness.

_____
_____
_____
_____
_____
_____
_____
_____

Prayer

"Dear Lord,
I come before You with a heavy heart, seeking healing for the friendship that has broken. I ask that You give me the strength to forgive and the wisdom to understand the journey my friend and I are on. Help us to rebuild what has been lost or to find peace in letting go if that is Your will. Guide our hearts with grace, patience and love, and may our paths be aligned with Your purpose.
In Jesus' name,
Amen."

GIRL, IT'S TIME TO HEAL

GIRL, IT'S TIME TO HEAL

Chapter 7: Mom & Dad
HEALING FROM FAMILY STRUGGLES

> *Reflecting on Family Addictions*
> *Psalm 34:17: "Is anyone crying for help? God is listening, ready to rescue you."*
> *Growing up with parents who had addictions can be emotionally challenging. Acknowledge how those struggles affected your childhood.*

Reflect on how your parents' struggles with gambling and work addiction shaped your early life. How did it impact your responsibilities as a child?

_____
_____
_____

> *Coping with Responsibility*
> *Proverbs 22:6: "Point your kids in the right direction; when they're old, they won't be lost."*

Many children take on adult responsibilities when their parents are unable to. Recognizing and processing these experiences can be healing.

What responsibilities did you take on as a child? How did it shape your understanding of family and support?

_____
_____
_____

> ***Understanding Redemption***
> 2 Corinthians 5:17: *"Now we look inside, and what we see is that anyone united with the Messiah gets a fresh start, is created new. The old life is gone; a new life emerges!"*

Your father's transformation through faith was a pivotal moment for your family. Reflect on how this change impacted your family dynamics.

How did your father's decision to give his life to Christ change the way your family functioned? How did this affect your own faith or outlook on life?

_____
_____
_____

> ***Rebuilding Trust and Stability***
> Isaiah 43:19: *"Be alert, be present. I'm about to do something brand new. It's bursting out! Don't you see it? There it is! I'm making a road through the desert, rivers in the Badlands."*

As your father rebuilt his business and your family regained balance, reflect on the journey from instability to stability.

What was the most challenging aspect of your family's struggles? How did you and your family rebuild trust and stability after those tough times?

_____
_____
_____
_____

> **Exploring Forgiveness**
> *Ephesians 4:32:* *"Be gentle with one another, sensitive. Forgive one another as quickly and thoroughly as God in Christ forgave you."*

Forgiving family members for their shortcomings or mistakes can be hard, but it is essential for healing.

Have you found forgiveness for your parents' addictions and the impact they had on your childhood? How can you work towards deeper forgiveness for them or others?

_____

_____

_____

> **Finding Strength in Resilience**
> *Philippians 4:13:* *"Whatever I have, wherever I am, I can make it through anything in the one who makes me who I am."*

Despite the challenges, your family showed resilience in the face of adversity. God gives strength to move forward and overcome.

What strengths have you developed from your family's struggles? How can you use those strengths to help others facing similar challenges?

_____

_____

_____

_____

Prayer is a powerful tool to seek healing and restoration for yourself and your family.

Write a prayer for continued healing and restoration in your family and for others who may be facing similar challenges.

_____
_____
_____
_____
_____
_____
_____
_____
_____

Prayer

Dear Lord,
I thank You for Your constant love and faithfulness, even in the midst of difficult family situations. I ask for healing for myself and my family, that we may continue to grow in faith and love. Help us to overcome any remaining struggles and to find peace and restoration through Your grace. Let us always remember that You are with us through every trial, guiding us toward hope and renewal.
In Jesus' name,
Amen.

GIRL, IT'S TIME TO HEAL

GIRL, IT'S TIME TO HEAL

Chapter 8: Puppies
HEALING FROM CHILDHOOD TRAUMA

> *Acknowledging the Pain*
> *Psalm 147:3:* "He heals the heartbroken and bandages their wounds."

The pain of trauma can leave scars that feel permanent, but the first step in healing is acknowledging the pain and allowing yourself to feel it.

Reflect on your earliest memories of the trauma you've faced. What emotions do you associate with these memories?

_____

_____

_____

> *Understanding Trauma's Impact*
> *Romans 8:28:* "That's why we can be sure that every detail in our lives of love for God is worked into something good."

Reflection: Trauma doesn't only affect us emotionally but can change our perceptions of self-worth and relationships.

How did this experience make you feel about yourself?

_____

_____

_____

_____

How did it affect your relationships with others?

_____
_____
_____

Helpful Tool: List three affirmations you can remind yourself of each day to help rebuild your self-worth.

_____
_____
_____

> **The Role of Shame and Silence**
> *Isaiah 61:7: "Because you got a double dose of trouble and more than your share of contempt, your inheritance in the land will be doubled and your joy go on forever."*
> *Reflection*

Shame often keeps people silent about their trauma, causing years of suffering in isolation.

Why do you think you stayed silent about your trauma for so long?

_____
_____
_____

How has carrying the weight of silence impacted your life?

_____
_____
_____

Helpful Tool: Write down three reasons why speaking up about your pain is important for your healing.

_____

_____

_____

> *Breaking the Silence*
> *Proverbs 18:21: "Words kill, words give life; they're either poison or fruit; you choose."*
> *Time to Reflect*

Speaking up about your trauma is difficult but necessary to begin healing.

Who can you trust to share your story with?

_____

_____

_____

What steps can you take to start talking about your experience?

_____

_____

_____

Helpful Tool: Create a support circle — list three people you can talk to when you need support.

_____

_____

_____

> **Releasing the Burden**
> *Matthew 11:28: "Are you tired? Worn out? Burned out on religion? Come to me. Get away with me and you'll recover your life."*

Time to Reflect

Releasing the burden of trauma is crucial for healing and finding peace.

What burdens are you carrying that you need to release?

_____
_____
_____

How can you start letting go of these weights?

_____
_____
_____

Helpful Tool: Write a letter to yourself expressing your intention to release these burdens and embrace peace.

_____
_____
_____
_____
_____
_____

Prayer

Psalm 147:3, Romans 8:28, Isaiah 61:7, Proverbs 18:21, Matthew 11:28

Heavenly Father,
I come to You today with a heart that longs for healing. The pain from my past has held me down, but I trust in Your power to restore and renew. Help me release the burdens I've carried for so long — burdens of shame, fear and unforgiveness. Guide me through this journey of healing, one step at a time. Teach me to forgive, to love myself again, and to trust that You have a plan for my restoration. Cover me in Your peace and remind me that through You, all things are made new. Thank You for the strength to face my past and for the hope of a brighter future.
In Jesus' name,
Amen.

GIRL, IT'S TIME TO HEAL

GIRL, IT'S TIME TO HEAL

Chapter 9: Phat Girl
HEALING YOUR RELATIONSHIP WITH BODY IMAGE

> **Understanding the Root**
> *Psalm 139:14: "I thank you, High God; you're breathtaking! Body and soul, I am marvelously made! I worship in adoration; what a creation!"*

Reflect on your earliest memories of your body and your relationship with food.

When did you start noticing your weight, and how did it make you feel?

_____
_____
_____

How have your thoughts about your body evolved over time?

_____
_____
_____

> **Confronting the Past**
> *Philippians 3:13-14: "Friends, don't get me wrong: by no means do I count myself an expert in all of this, but I've got my eye on the goal, where God is beckoning us onward; to Jesus. I'm off and running, and I'm not turning back."*

What messages or experiences from your childhood shaped how you see yourself today?

_____

_____

_____

Write down moments when you felt insecure or judged because of your weight.

_____

_____

_____

How did those experiences affect your self-esteem and relationships with others?

_____

_____

_____

> **Breaking Free from Shame**
> *Romans 8:1: "With the arrival of Jesus, the Messiah, that fateful dilemma is resolved."*

Shame often keeps us trapped in cycles of unhealthy behavior. Write about any shame or guilt you've carried regarding your body.

_____

_____

_____

How have you internalized others' comments or judgments?

_____
_____
_____

What steps can you take to release that shame and walk confidently in your identity?

_____
_____
_____

> *Setting Goals for Health and Wholeness*
> *1 Corinthians 6:19–20:* "Don't you see that you can't live however you please, squandering what God paid such a high price for? The physical part of you is not some piece of property belonging to the spiritual part of you. God owns the whole works so let people see God in and through your body."

What are your health goals moving forward? Be specific about physical, emotional and spiritual well-being. Write down one goal in each of these areas:

Physical: What are some healthy habits you can commit to?

_____
_____
_____

Emotional: How can you nurture your mental and emotional health?

_____

_____

_____

Spiritual: What spiritual practices will help you see your body as a temple of God?

_____

_____

_____

Time for Setting Goals

> *Prayer for Healing and Strength*
> *Isaiah 40:31 (NIV): "But those who wait upon God get fresh strength. They spread their wings and sore like eagles, they run and don't get tired, they walk and don't lag behind."*

Reflect on what you've learned through this process. What will you do differently in the future?

_____

_____

_____

_____

_____

Write a personal prayer asking for strength and perseverance in your journey to wholeness.

_____

_____

_____

Prayer

Dear Heavenly Father,

I thank You for creating me wonderfully in Your image. I have carried burdens of shame and insecurity for too long, but today I release them into Your hands. Help me to honor my body as the temple You designed it to be. Give me the strength and discipline to care for it physically, mentally and spiritually. When I struggle, remind me of Your love and grace. Help me to set healthy goals and see myself as You see me — worthy, loved and precious. Thank You for Your healing power in my life.

In Jesus' name,

Amen.

GIRL, IT'S TIME TO HEAL

GIRL, IT'S TIME TO HEAL

Chapter 10: Family Secrets
REFLECTING ON THE PAST, A NEW BEGINNING AND GOAL SETTING

> *Ephesians 4:28:* "*Did you used to make ends meet by stealing? Well, no more! Get an honest job so that you can help others who can't work.*"

Reflect on what led to your decisions in the past and how you felt during those moments. What were the emotions driving your actions?

_____
_____
_____

How did these decisions affect your relationships, self-image and faith?

_____
_____
_____

Journal Your Thoughts

Goal Setting: What steps can you take to ensure you walk with integrity moving forward?

_____
_____
_____

Write down one or two concrete goals related to financial integrity, self-worth or healing from past mistakes.

Goal 1

_____
_____

Goal 2

_____
_____

> **A New Beginning**
> *Proverbs 28:13: "You can't whitewash your sins and get by with it; you find mercy by admitting and leaving them."*

How can you rely on God's grace to move forward from the mistakes of your past?

_____
_____
_____

What does forgiveness — both giving and receiving — look like in your current life?

_____
_____
_____

Time to reflect on forgiveness and grace.

Prayer

Dear Heavenly Father,

I thank You for Your mercy and grace that cover my life. I confess my past mistakes and ask for Your help to walk in integrity and righteousness. Heal my heart from the shame and guilt of my past, and help me trust in Your forgiveness. Guide me in making honest decisions and showing grace to others. Lord, I ask for strength to achieve the goals I've set and to live in a way that reflects Your love and truth.
In Jesus' name,
Amen.

Acknowledging the Pain
Psalm 34:18: "*If your heart is broken, you'll find God right there; if you're kicked in the gut, He'll help you catch your breath.*"

Reflect on the feelings of guilt, anger and betrayal after discovering what happened to your child. How has this affected your relationship with family, your sense of trust and your faith?

_____

_____

_____

Goal Setting
Goal 1: Identify a specific emotion you need to work through.

_____

_____

Goal 2: Write down one step you can take to begin processing that emotion (e.g., speaking with a counselor, journaling daily or praying for peace).

_____

_____

> **Breaking the Silence**
> Luke 8:17: "We are not keeping secrets; we're telling them. We're not hiding things; we're bringing everything out into the open."

Consider how the silence and secrecy around your son's abuse affected the healing process. Why is it important to speak up about abuse, even when it involves family members?

_____

_____

_____

Goal 1: Write down one person you can trust to talk to about the abuse or one way you can break the silence (e.g., joining a support group or writing a letter).

_____

_____

Goal 2: Identify one way you can create a safer environment for your family (e.g., open communication, setting boundaries).

_____

_____

> **Seeking Help and Counseling**
> Proverbs 11:14: "Without good direction, people lose their way; the more wise counsel you follow, the better your chances.

How could seeking professional help have supported both you and your son through this painful experience?

_____

_____

_____

What fears or obstacles have prevented you from seeking counseling before?

_____

_____

_____

Time to Journal

> **Information on Counseling**
> Counseling can provide a safe space to process trauma, offer guidance on how to move forward, and help both you and your child heal. Licensed counselors, especially those who specialize in trauma, can work with you to break patterns of secrecy and help restore a sense of security. Consider reaching out to a counselor or therapist, and check if they have experience with childhood abuse cases.

Goal Setting
Goal 1: Research local or online counselors specializing in trauma.

_____

_____

Goal 2: Make an appointment for an initial consultation, or reach out to a support group for survivors of abuse.

_____

_____

Trusting God for Healing

Reflect on how you can trust God to heal the brokenness in your heart and your son's life.

How can you rely on His strength to rebuild trust and protect your family from further harm?

_____

_____

_____

Goal Setting
Goal 1: Spend time in prayer asking God to heal your heart and protect your family.

_____

_____

Goal 2: Write down one scripture you will meditate on during difficult moments.

_____

_____

> **Breaking Generational Curses**
> Exodus 34:7: "Still, He doesn't ignore sin. He holds sons and grandsons responsible for a father's sins to their third and even fourth generation."

How can you break the cycle of secrecy and abuse within your family?

_____

_____

_____

What steps can you take to protect future generations from the same pain?

_____

_____

_____

Prayer for Healing from Stealing and Sexual Assault

Dear Lord,
I come to You with a heavy heart, seeking Your mercy and guidance. I ask for Your strength to overcome the habit of stealing that I know dishonors You and harms others. Help me find peace in doing what is right and trust that You will provide for my every need. Give me the courage to break free from this destructive path and to walk in integrity.
Lord, I also ask for Your healing touch upon the deep wounds of my past. Heal me from the trauma and pain of sexual assault, restoring my spirit and mind. Help me to find peace, love and strength in Your arms, knowing that You see me as whole and worthy. Surround me with Your protection and guide me as I seek healing and restoration.
In Jesus' name,
Amen.

GIRL, IT'S TIME TO HEAL

GIRL, IT'S TIME TO HEAL

Chapter 11: Keep Dreaming
REDISCOVERING YOUR DREAM

> *Jeremiah 29:11: "I know what I'm doing. I have it all planned out; plans to take care of you, not abandon you, plans to give you the future you hope for."*

Reflect on your early dreams. What was your childhood dream?

_____
_____
_____

How did life circumstances cause you to lose sight of that dream?

_____
_____
_____

Goal Setting
Goal 1: Write down one dream or goal you want to revisit.

_____
_____

Goal 2: Identify one action you can take to start pursuing that dream again.

_____

_____

> ***Overcoming Negative Voices***
> *Proverbs 18:21: "Words kill, words give life; they're either poison or fruit; you choose."*

Think about a time when someone's words discouraged you from pursuing your goals.

How did their words impact you?

_____

_____

_____

What will you do differently now?

_____

_____

_____

Goal Setting
Goal 1: Write down one way you will silence negative voices in your life.

_____

_____

Goal 2: Identify one person who encourages and supports your dreams. How can you rely on their support?

_____

_____

> **Embracing Your Gifts**
> *1 Peter 4:10: "Be generous with the different things God gave you, passing them around so all you get in on it: if words, let it be God's words; if help, let it be God's heart help."*

Reflect on the gifts and talents God has given you. What abilities do you have that can help you achieve your goals?

_____

_____

_____

Goal Setting
Goal 1: Write down one of your unique talents and how you plan to use it.

_____

_____

Goal 2: Set a short-term goal to develop that talent further.

_____

_____

> **Trusting God in Your Journey**
> *Proverbs 3:5–6: "Trust God from the bottom of your heart; don't try to figure out everything on your own. Listen for God's voice in everything you do, everywhere you go; He's the one who will keep you on track."*

Consider how God has guided you through difficult situations in the past. How can you trust Him with your dreams moving forward?

_____

_____

_____

Goal Setting
Goal 1: Identify a challenge or setback in pursuing your dream. Write down how you can trust God to guide you through it.

_____

_____

Goal 2: Write down one way you can submit your plans to God and trust His timing.

_____

_____

Prayer

Heavenly Father,

You have placed desires and dreams in my heart, and I come to You now seeking the strength to keep moving forward. Sometimes, I feel weary or uncertain, but I know that with You, I can reignite my passion and creativity. Breathe new life into my soul, Lord. Open my mind to fresh ideas, my heart to new dreams and my spirit to greater purpose. Help me to trust in Your timing and not lose hope when the journey is hard. Remind me that the gifts You have given me are meant to flourish. Fill me with Your energy, peace and inspiration so that I can continue to create and dream in ways that bring glory to You.
In Jesus' name,
Amen.

Your dreams and creativity are valuable, and you have the strength to keep going!

GIRL, IT'S TIME TO HEAL

GIRL, IT'S TIME TO HEAL